DIGGER DIGGER DIGGER

Written by
Mark A. Clarke

Illustrated by
Karen Amendolagine

Copyright © 2022 Mark A. Clarke

No portion of this book may be reproduced or used in any form, or by any means, without prior written permission of the author.

Cover illustration by Karen Amendolagine
Cover and book design by Cindy Casey

Published by
CCE PUBLISHING
Edgewater, Florida

Printed in the United Sates of America

ISBN 978-1-7373017-2-1 (Paperback)

Dedication

To Jeff and Karen

Written by
Mark A. Clarke

Illustrated by
Karen Amendolagine

CCE PUBLISHING
EDGEWATER, FLORIDA

Digger Digger Digger,
Big Scoop Dump!
Elliot barely four
Gave his other foot a stomp.

Toys were his passion,
Like the grader and the truck,
But the digger was his favorite,
When digging in the muck.

Digger Digger Digger,
Big Scoop Dump!
"Whoopee for the Digger!"
He shouted with a jump.

Digger Digger Digger,
Big Scoop Dump!
Raising up his other arm,
He gave his fist a pump.

Deeper in the dirt,
Steady he would dig,
Down, deep and pleasing
The hole grew ever big.

Digger Digger Digger,
Big Scoop Dump!
The mound of sand grew higher,
like a dromedary's hump.

Tall, tan and delightful,
Sand piled in his box,
When he ran out of soil
He started with some rocks.

So, his digger dug and dug.
"I must dig and dig," he said.

Till his mother came that evening,
And took him off to bed.

Digger ... Digger ... Digger ...
Big ... Scoop ... Dump ...

He mumbled and he muttered,
While lying in a clump.

I'll dig… and dig… and dig…
till…the hole… is big… and deep…

Author Acknowledgments

I would like to thank my wife Susan, who with her patience and insight helped me to articulate language into precise thoughts.

I appreciate Karen Amendolagine for her creative insight and talent with painting the written word into a work of art.

I would be remiss if I did not mention my editor, Cindy Casey. She and I have a shared love of language and educational experience, (Syracuse University). She is the literary glue that is necessary with uniting words and language into a cogent story.

Finally, I would like to thank a young boy by the name of Elliot Hewitt. It was his genuine simplicity that inspired this story and allowed me to breathe, once again, the refreshing air of my youth with *Mike Mulligan and His Steam Shovel*.

About the Author

Mark A. Clarke grew up in Upstate New York. Enlisting in the United States Army during the Vietnam War, he served in an Airborne Infantry Regiment in Europe. Mark earned a bachelor's degree in English Education at SUNY Oswego, a master's degree at Saint Rose and post graduate studies in a PhD program at Syracuse University.

Studying Anglo-American literature for a semester in London, he met and discussed the works of Kingsley Amis, Ruth Fainlight and Gordon M. Williams. Mark taught for more than thirty years in a public school in Columbia County, where he met his wife.

His first book was *Columbia: Those Who Honorably Served*, which recounted the lives and service of 200 veterans from Columbia County. His second book, *Harriet's Egg,* is an enchanting children's story about kindness, determination, and the power of motherly love. *Digger, Digger, Digger* is Mark's third book and *Black River*, a collection of short stories to be published in the fall, his fourth.

About the Illustrator

Karen Amendolagine is a traditional artist, specializing in graphite, colored pencil, oils and watercolor. As art is in her DNA, she began private lessons in her adolescence. During her later years in high school, she began displaying work at Bethlehem Art Gallery in Cornwall, New York.

After earning her Bachelor of Fine Arts from Salisbury University in Maryland, Karen continued exhibiting her work in small galleries and cafés in Tokyo, Japan, and at Beyond the Lines Gallery and The Hive Gallery in Los Angeles, California, along with multiple pop-up shows around the city.

Karen also illustrated Mark A. Clarke's first children's book, *Harriet's Egg*. In 2020 she illustrated her first children's book, *The Real & Curious You: A Childhood to Adulthood Learning Guide*.

Karen continues to grow her body of work in Queens, New York.

Reader Accolades for Mark A. Clarke's
DIGGER DIGGER DIGGER

Digger Digger Digger, Big Scoop Dump...love the repetitive text! I love books that are interactive and allow the child to participate!! I love that you used the word dromedary instead of camel. A new word for my grandson to learn and use!

Linda Radewitz

Parent

I LOVE this one. I will be ordering a copy once it's ready to use with my kindergartners! I like some of the higher-level language which will be useful in teaching my ELLs some of the more colorful words in our English language.

Paul Caswell

Teacher

Digger Digger Digger is a unique story for children. The beginning immediately draws the child into the book. The character is likeable and one that children will easily relate to as the story progresses. What child with sandbox toys wouldn't want to hear this story? There is an excellent balance between the vivid, colorful illustrations and the text.

Julie Veronezi

Teacher

This is great! I see it being very engaging for young children, especially those who like to dig in the dirt. I love the rhyming because it is not the usual rhyme pattern you find in children's books: cat/rat, fun/sun, etc. It opens the door for a lot of discussion with the vocabulary as well.

Leah Prack

Elementary teacher

One of my fondest memories as a child was playing and digging in the dirt. One of the first things I built for my sons was a sandbox in which we spent hours digging, building roads and making powerful engine sounds. This brought back all those memories! I love it!

Pat Wemett
Teacher/administrator

This kind of rhyme is very appealing to young children, and they often request the story to be read over and over again, sometimes to the point of memorizing some or all of it, or even singing the words. ...Children will enjoy this book as a read-aloud, and especially those who enjoy digging in the dirt or sand, in backyard or beach.

Kathy Allen
PhD Education

I looked at the book as if I was reading it to my library story hour children (ages 1 to 4 years) All of whom have little or no attention span. The illustrations are colorful with a lot going on – helpful to keep their attention. The illustrations lend themselves to easy discussion and relating to own experiences. The subject is great – both the girls and boys love to play with the small trucks and cars in the library, so they can certainly relate to Elliot.

Debbie Wiede
Elementary teacher

Very cute. I have younger grandnieces and know they could relate to this story as well as boys. It is an activity that many children have experienced. The pictures go nicely with your words.

Anne Matson
Teacher

Also by Mark A. Clarke

- COLUMBIA: Those Who Honorably Served
  June 2021
- Harriet's Egg
  December 2021
- Black River: Tales of the North Country
  Autumn 2022

Made in the USA
Coppell, TX
14 February 2023